FIRE's GUIDE TO
FIRST-YEAR ORIENTATION AND
THOUGHT REFORM ON CAMPUS

FIRE's GUIDES TO
STUDENT RIGHTS ON CAMPUS
www.thefireguides.org

FIRE's Guide to Religious Liberty on Campus

FIRE's Guide to Student Fees, Funding, and Legal Equality
on Campus

FIRE's Guide to Due Process and Fair Procedure on Campus

FIRE's Guide to Free Speech on Campus

FIRE's Guide to First-Year Orientation and
Thought Reform on Campus

FIRE

David French
President

FIRE's GUIDE TO

FIRST-YEAR ORIENTATION AND THOUGHT REFORM ON CAMPUS

Harvey A. Silverglate
Jordan Lorence

FOUNDATION FOR INDIVIDUAL RIGHTS IN EDUCATION
Philadelphia

Library of Congress Cataloging-in-Publication Data

Silverglate, Harvey A., 1942-
   FIRE's guide to first-year orientation and thought reform on campus /
Harvey A. Silverglate, Jordan Lorence.
      p. cm. — (FIRE's guides to students' rights on campus)
   Includes bibliographical references.
   ISBN 0-9724712-3-5 (alk. paper)
   1. Freedom of expression—United States. 2. College students—Civil
rights—United States. 3. Political correctness—United States. I. Title:
Guide to first-year orientation and thought reform on campus. II. Lorence,
Jordan. III. Title. IV. FIRE's guides to student rights on campus
   KF4770.S575 2005
   378.1'98'0973—dc22

                                                                    2005019425

Published in the United States of America by:

      Foundation for Individual Rights in Education
      601 Walnut Street, Suite 510
      Philadelphia, PA 19106

Cover art printed by permission of Patrick Whelan
Cover and interior design by Yoonsun Chung
Printed in the United States of America

ACKNOWLEDGMENTS

FIRE's *Guides* to Student Rights on Campus are made possible by contributions from thousands of individual donors and by grants from:

The Achelis and Bodman Foundations
Aequus Institute
Earhart Foundation
Pierre F. and Enid Goodrich Foundation
The Joseph Harrison Jackson Foundation
John Templeton Foundation

FIRE gratefully acknowledges their generous support.

For information about contributing to FIRE's efforts, please visit www.thefire.org/support.

CONTENTS

PREFACE

"We are not content with negative obedience, nor even with the most abject submission. When finally you surrender to us, it must be of your own free will. We do not destroy the heretic....We convert him, we capture his inner mind, we reshape him....You must love Big Brother. It is not enough to obey him; you must love him."—O'Brien to Winston, in George Orwell, *1984*

"Struggles to coerce uniformity of sentiment in support of some end thought essential to their time and country have been waged by many good, as well as by evil, men. Nationalism is a relatively recent phenomenon, but, at other times and places, the ends have been racial or territorial security, support of a dynasty or regime, and particular plans for saving souls. As first and moderate methods to attain unity have failed, those bent on its

accomplishment must resort to an ever-increasing sever-
ity. As governmental pressure toward unity becomes
greater, so strife becomes more bitter as to whose unity
it shall be. Probably no deeper division of our people
could proceed from any provocation than from finding it
necessary to choose what doctrine and whose program
public educational officials shall compel youth to unite in
embracing. Ultimate futility of such attempts to compel
coherence is the lesson of every such effort from the
Roman drive to stamp out Christianity as a disturber of
its pagan unity, the Inquisition, as a means to religious
and dynastic unity, the Siberian exiles as a means to
Russian unity, down to the fast failing efforts of our present totalitarian enemies. Those who begin coercive elimi-
nation of dissent soon find themselves exterminating
dissenters. Compulsory unification of opinion achieves
only the unanimity of the graveyard."—*The Supreme
Court of the United States, in West Virginia State Board of
Education v. Barnette* (1943)

INTRODUCTION: THE INDISPENSABLE RIGHT TO PRIVATE CONSCIENCE

Support for freewheeling debate and the freedom to challenge reigning assumptions are the cornerstones of our American culture of rights, our constitutional order, designed to defend that culture, and our system of higher education. The freedom to disagree, to state one's beliefs and values, and to discuss and argue peacefully makes democratic deliberation possible and allows us to pursue truth unfettered by the demands of any one ideology or orthodox point of view. As John Stuart Mill wrote in *On Liberty*, "[T]he peculiar evil of silencing the expression of an opinion is, that it is robbing the human race; posterity as well as the existing generation, those who dissent from the opinion, still more than those who hold it. If the opinion is right, they are deprived of the opportunity of exchanging error for truth: if wrong, they lose, what is almost as great a benefit, the clearer perception and livelier impression of truth, produced by its collision with error."

This right to free expression is enshrined in the First Amendment to the United States Constitution, which bars the government (including administrators at state colleges and universities) from enacting any law that serves to prevent a citizen, including a student, from speaking his or her mind, with very limited exceptions (for example, obscenity, libel or slander, incitement to imminent violence, or threats). Thus, for example, a citizen who wishes to express his or her support for or opposition to the nation's foreign policy may not be stopped from doing so. (For a more detailed discussion of this topic of free speech, see *FIRE's Guide to Free Speech on Campus.*)

Before one can have the freedom to express ideas in open debate, however, one must have freedom of conscience: the right to arrive at one's private beliefs, without being coerced into an artificial unity by those who wield power over us. After all, the freedom to speak is a dead letter if one lacks the freedom to think, to believe, or to disbelieve. At the heart of American liberty lies a recognition of individual rights, individual responsibility, and individual dignity. Over one's inner mind, conscience, and self, no one has coercive power.

There is, of course, an interaction between freedom of conscience and belief, on the one hand, and freedom of speech, on the other. Usually when one speaks, one is expressing what one believes. Although belief and speech are, in one sense, two sides of the same coin, there is, nonetheless, an important distinction between them. When the government seeks to *prevent* someone from speaking his or her mind, that is what we traditionally call *censorship*. Censorship is generally a dreadful thing, but coercing belief and conscience is yet more pernicious and evil, because it invades the inner being of an individual's life. Sometimes tyrannical power seeks to *force* individuals under its sway to *speak or utter* things that the speaker does *not* believe. In our moral tradition, that is a frightful assault upon the innermost sanctum of human privacy and dignity. In our legal tradition, it is a worse violation of the First Amendment to force someone to say that which he does not believe (which we might describe as an *affirmative* form of censorship) than to prevent him from saying that which he does believe (which we might describe as a *negative* form of censorship).

The form of censorship with which this *Guide* is concerned is the affirmative form of censorship that goes beyond prohibiting "bad" speech and ideas. It instead seeks to impose on a student, and coerce the student to adopt, and to believe in, the "approved" point of view advanced by the authorities. Official acts that invade this private sphere of thought and conscience—what we call, in its starkest form, "thought reform"—are related to the more familiar concept of censorship of public speech, but reach far deeper. Instead of preventing students from *expressing* their views and beliefs, thought reform seeks to coerce students into *contradicting* those views and beliefs by saying things that they do not believe and that may, in fact, violate their most deeply held beliefs, with the ultimate goal of forcing change in those beliefs themselves. This act reaches deep into the mind and heart of a human being and seeks to force him not only to abandon his own beliefs, but also to mouth and indeed adopt the beliefs of those in positions of power and authority over him.

Censoring speech is bad enough, but requiring people to adhere to, and even to believe (or at least to proclaim belief) in an official, orthodox ideology is completely incompatible with a free society and is the hallmark of totalitarian social control. Of course, those who endeavor to force others to believe in an official ideology and who punish the expression of dissent frequently do so under the guise of enforcing "good," "moral," and "ethical" values and social goals. When a government or administration seeks to force those under its authority to believe and to mouth certain views, that authority claims to be implementing positive values—"politically correct," as the phrase goes—leading to the good society. For those who would coerce thought, belief, and conscience, dissent from their own point of view is evil or immoral or antisocial, and not simply the expression of a different point of view.

History should have taught us to hold in horror the violation of conscience and private belief. The "peat bog soldiers," Nazi prisoners sent to work in the fields until they died, sang the song, *"Die Gedanken sind frei,"* "Thoughts Are Free." Inward thoughts and convictions truly are the final atoms of human liberty. No decent institution, civilization, or person pursues an unwilling fellow creature there. Our colleges and universities do so routinely.

The fundamental rights of conscience and belief, the thought-reform programs that threaten those rights at today's universities, and the means by which a decent and free people can challenge such programs are the topics of this *Guide*.

PROTECTION OF CONSCIENCE: *West Virginia State Board of Education v. Barnette* (1943)

The concept of the First Amendment's protection of the freedom of conscience and deterrence against official attempts to engage in "thought reform" of its citizens, is best exemplified by the opinion of the Supreme Court in the landmark 1943 case of *West Virginia State Board of Education v. Barnette.*[1]

America was at war with totalitarian powers in 1943. It was not yet clear what the outcome of that war would be, although the Allied Powers were doing better than in the earliest years of the conflict. Still, the fates of the Western democracies, including the United States, were

---

[1]The authors wish to acknowledge here the discussion of this case in Alan Charles Kors and Harvey A. Silverglate, *The Shadow University: The Betrayal of Liberty on America's Campuses* (The Free Press, 1998; paperback edition from HarperPerennial, 1999), portions of which have been liberally quoted here. We have made liberal use as well of *The Shadow University*'s discussion of other cases.

hanging in the balance. The West Virginia legislature, expressing a desire to aid the national war effort against European fascism, had enacted a statute to require all public and private schools to teach, foster, and perpetuate "the ideas, principles and spirit of Americanism." The state Board of Education ordered a daily flag salute. Refusal subjected the student to dismissal and subjected parents to criminal penalties.

Several members of the Jehovah's Witnesses religion—parents and their children—objected to participating in the flag salute, believing that to pledge to a flag was an act of idolatry, a form of bowing to graven images, prohibited by the Old Testament. They did not object to others pledging, but they refused to do so themselves. In *West Virginia State Board of Education v. Barnette*, the Supreme Court analyzed the constitutionality of such a requirement not solely in terms of religious liberty but, more broadly, in terms of the right of private conscience against governmental coercion of expressions of belief and loyalty. Writing for the majority, Justice Robert Jackson had no quarrel with West Virginia's requirement that certain courses be *taught*, nor with its attempts to *inspire* patriotism by *exposing* students to national history and traditions. However, in the Court's view the Board's flag salute requirement was different, because it *compelled* a student "to declare a belief [and]...to utter what is not in his mind." In matters of belief, the Court saw human beings as essentially distinct;

each was free to find "jest and scorn" where another found "comfort and inspiration."

The Court found that the underlying issue was not any claimed conflict between liberty of conscience and the state's ability to survive in time of crisis. The issue was not weak versus strong government, but, rather, seeing the strength of America in "individual freedom of mind" rather than in "officially disciplined uniformity for which history indicates a disappointing and disastrous end." Enforced conformity, far from teaching the value of liberty, would "strangle the free mind at its source and teach youth to discount important principles of our government as mere platitudes."

Justice Jackson explained why even men of good intentions should not possess the awesome power to compel belief. Both the good and the evil had attempted "to coerce uniformity of sentiment in support of some end thought essential." Such goals had been variously racial, territorial, and religious, but each such effort, Jackson reasoned, raised the bitter and profoundly divisive question of "whose unity it shall be." Nothing, ultimately, would divide society more than "finding it necessary to choose what doctrine and whose program public educational officials shall compel youth to unite in embracing." Surely all of human history taught the "ultimate futility of such attempts to compel coherence," as seen in Roman efforts to destroy Christianity, the Inquisition's attempt to ensure religious unity, and "the

Siberian exiles as a means to Russian unity, down to the fast failing efforts of our present totalitarian enemies." In short, Jackson wrote for the majority of the Court, "compulsory unification of opinion achieves only the unanimity of the graveyard." He concluded: "It seems trite but necessary to say that the First Amendment to our Constitution was designed to avoid these ends by avoiding these beginnings."

For the Court, arguments that wartime and patriotism raised singular problems constituted "an unflattering estimate of the appeal of our institutions to free minds." Without the toleration of eccentricity and "abnormal attitudes," we could not have either our treasured "intellectual individualism" or our "rich cultural diversities." It would violate the very spirit of liberty to make an exception for coercion of what society found to be its most important beliefs. The "freedom to differ is not limited to things that do not matter much," the Court wrote: "That would be a mere shadow of freedom. The test of its substance is the right to differ as to things that touch the heart of the existing order."

Justice Jackson concluded with a particularly eloquent refutation of claims for the value of enforced orthodoxy in civic life. His words addressed issues that lie at the heart of the links among the First Amendment, academic freedom, and the right of individuals to define their deepest sense of themselves. "If there is any fixed star in our constitutional constellation," he wrote, "it is that no official, high or petty, can prescribe what shall be orthodox in politics, nationalism, religion, or other matters of opinion or force citizens to confess by words or act their faith" in such orthodoxy. "The purpose of the First Amendment to our Constitution," he concluded, was precisely to protect "from all official control" the domain that was "the sphere of intellect and spirit." Thus was confirmed the primacy of individual conscience over the perceived social benefits of conformity, the need for each individual to enjoy liberty in order for a common liberty to exist, and the intolerability of restricting even one person's liberty in "the sphere of intellect and spirit" in an attempt to create some better world or even a better human race.

CAMPUS ATTEMPTS TO REFORM AND DICTATE BELIEFS AND ATTITUDES

Students entering colleges and universities deserve a rich intellectual environment where they find themselves invited into freewheeling debates, with many, many different voices, on a wide range of important topics. Unfortunately, many colleges today behave, instead, like "enclaves of totalitarianism," a term that the Supreme Court coined to describe violations of free speech in high schools, in the case of *Tinker v. Des Moines Independent Community School District* (1969). If secondary schools, which educate children, are prohibited from becoming totalitarian, colleges and universities, which educate adults, are held to a much higher standard. Unfortunately, these institutions all too often betray their obligation to honor diversity of opinion, freedom of conscience, open debate, and the free marketplace of ideas. As one can see in abundance on the website of the

13

Foundation for Individual Rights in Education (FIRE), college officials frequently suppress ideas and speakers with whom they disagree, and use coercive tactics that violate the individual rights of students to formulate their own beliefs. (See www.thefire.org.)

Methods of enforcing officially approved points of view go beyond mere censorship. Campuses often adopt an official orthodoxy on matters of politics, values, and worldview, and they try to force students to mouth and even to believe the points of view that the administrators believe to be appropriately progressive or "politically correct." These methods of thought reform include:

- Mandatory diversity "training" that aims to intimidate students into abandoning deeply held beliefs so that they will adopt the university's preferred political stance. The distinction between "education" and "training" or "indoctrination" is important. While it is permissible, indeed valuable, to educate students about controversial issues and views of race, sex, and sexuality in our society, the university has no right to coerce students into adopting only one approved point of view on these issues.

- Ideologically tilted speech codes that privilege one point of view over others. Although civility codes that are neutral among competing viewpoints (that is, codes that control the manner in which a thought is expressed, but that don't seek to control the content of thought itself) also offend the First Amendment, ideologically biased codes and double standards infringe terribly on freedom of conscience by silencing individuals selectively. (The courts are harsher on censorship that seeks to outlaw a particular point of view than they are on censorship that attacks, instead, the form of the expression, even though the latter is also protected.) One example of such codes is that of Shippensburg University, whose rules FIRE successfully challenged in a 2003 lawsuit. The Shippensburg code stated, "Shippensburg University's commitment to racial tolerance, cultural diversity and social justice will *require* every member of this community to ensure that the principles of these ideals be mirrored in their *attitudes and behaviors*." (Emphasis added.) Similarly, FIRE has criticized professors who compel students to sign statements agreeing to certain viewpoints or behaviors in order to limit debate to "acceptable" viewpoints.

• The use of nondiscrimination policies as a weapon to expel from campus or to suppress certain student groups that dissent from administrative campus orthodoxy, such as (these days) conservative religious groups, who often disagree with the college's stance on social issues such as gay rights and abortion. (At other periods of our history, of course, conservative religious groups were more in favor, while other more liberal groups were more out of favor. The pendulum of oppression usually swings, which is why it is so crucial to agree to protect individual rights not as a political tactic, but as a way of being human.) Although it is appropriate and important for the university to punish invidious forms of discrimination, it is wrong for the university to transform such neutral antidiscrimination enforcement responsibilities into a set of coercive double standards, an ideologically biased weapon that is applied selectively against certain groups.

• The imposition of mandatory psychological counseling, accountability training, or other forms of counseling as punishments for campus offenses. Often universities will agree to "leniency" for those accused of various campus offenses so long as the accused individuals agree to attend re-education sessions. Too many students agree to attend such sessions, mistakenly believing that it is not a form of "punishment" to sit through hours of coercive indoctrination.

Just as the framers of the First Amendment battled against the establishment of an official state-approved religion, a freedom contained in the First Amendment's religion clause, so does the First Amendment prevent the state from forcing citizens to believe, or mouth, an officially sanctioned point of view, whether political, philosophical, or personal. Free individuals disagree about and debate such views, and they seek to change each other's beliefs by persuasion and argument, not by coercion and force.

WHAT ABOUT PRIVATE COLLEGES AND UNIVERSITIES? A QUESTION OF ETHICS AND CONTRACT

Private universities and colleges stand in a different relation to the United States Constitution than governmental institutions such as public universities and colleges. The Bill of Rights of the Constitution imposes limits only on *governmental power* and action. Because a private college or university is not a governmental entity, it does not have to obey the First Amendment; it may, in other words, enforce speech restrictions upon its faculty and students that the government would not be permitted to enforce. The fact that a private institution is not bound by the Constitution, however, does not mean that it is not bound by the *rule of law*. Many private schools choose by their own formal and advertised policies to hold themselves to certain standards of freedom of speech, due process, diversity of opinion, and other concepts of academic freedom and protection of individual conscience. (Most private schools do not want to state that their students enjoy fewer rights of free speech and fairness than students at local public and community colleges.) A private school that enacts such policies may be required under state laws to live up to them. Many state laws exist to enforce contracts or outlaw fraud, appropriately requiring nonprofit institutions and businesses to live up to their own promises and advertised standards. These laws might compel a private school to respect the freedom of conscience of individual students or might prevent a private school from ordering a controversial student group disbanded because the school objects to the views expressed by the group. This model might apply to private universities and colleges that promote no distinct ideological or religious belief system, or, indeed, that promise certain standards of nondiscrimination, legal equality, and academic freedom.

Importantly, some states have laws (or state constitutional provisions) that provide students at private schools with some measure of First Amendment rights. For example, California's "Leonard Law" (Section 94367 of California's Education Code) states that "no private postsecondary educational institution shall make or enforce any rule subjecting any student to disciplinary sanctions solely on the basis of conduct that is speech or other communication that . . . is protected from governmental restriction by the First Amendment to the United States Constitution or Section 2 of Article 1 of the California Constitution." In other words, students at California's private, secular colleges and universities enjoy the same level of First Amendment rights as students at California's public colleges. The Leonard Law, however, does not apply to students at religious colleges, since the legislature was concerned not to interfere with the practice of religion.

In addition to those rights protected by contract and by statute, state law provides common-law rules against misrepresentation. Simply put, there is a long tradition of laws against fraud and deceit. Very often, a university's recruiting materials, brochures, and even its "admitted student" orientations—all of which are designed to entice a student to attend that institution rather than another—will loudly proclaim the school's commitment to "diversity," "inclusion," and "tolerance." Students will be assured that they will be "welcomed" or find a "home" on campus, regardless of their background or their religious or political viewpoints. Promises such as these might well lead students to say no to opportunities (and even scholarships) at other schools and to enroll in the private secular university. If these promises of "tolerance" or of a place in the community later turn out to be demonstrably false, or are delivered to some but withheld from others, a university could find itself in serious legal jeopardy. While private universities are rightfully beyond the reach of the Constitution, they have no license to deceive with false promise. A car dealer who deliberately promises six cylinders but delivers four breaks no Constitutional provision, but breaks many provisions of the common law and state statutes. Legal prohibitions against deceptive promises that dupe someone into signing a contract and legal prohibitions against false advertising can be used to force a change in a college administration's behavior.

By contrast, if a private college or university is organized around a specific set of ideological or political beliefs, then, in fact, the First Amendment protects its right to require students to conform to the college's set of beliefs. Students attending a private school established around a clear system of belief have no legal right to demand that the school allow dissenters to express conflicting views on campus. (If one attends an openly advertised Catholic seminary or Mormon college, for example, one has no legal grounds for challenging its specific mission.) The First Amendment's right of association protects the right of those private schools to promote their specific ideological or religious beliefs. Of course, a private college or university may not present itself as a secular liberal arts institution that guarantees a student's right to free expression but then, in practice, privilege and seek to impose a particular ideological or religious agenda by allowing only organizations that promote such an agenda to exist on campus. Such a practice would arguably violate the contractual obligation that the institution undertook when it promised its students a liberal arts education in which the free marketplace of ideas prevails. When a vendor advertises one product but then offers a different one in its place, that is known as "bait and switch." When a vendor claims to sell you one product but secretly substitutes another, that act is known as "fraud." Colleges and universities, too, may not with impunity engage in "bait and switch" or "fraud."

Moreover, when a private university violates students' freedom of conscience, they may meet all of their *legal* obligations but, in doing so, they violate their *moral* obligations to their students. In that situation, students can use the news media, advocacy organizations such as FIRE, and moral suasion to shame private university administrators into providing the same liberties to their students that they would receive at a public institution.

THE *BARNETTE* PRINCIPLE AND THE UNCONSTITUTIONALITY OF COERCING SOCIAL ATTITUDES

The *Barnette* case involved a situation in which a student, for *religious* reasons, refused to accept a *government* system of belief (or, in that case, the *symbol* of that system, namely the flag). Simply put, the student objected to the state's notion that patriotism, especially in time of war, is a sufficiently important value to be *enforced* in the minds, on the lips, and in the hearts of all citizens. As noted above, Justice Jackson's profound reasoning and powerful language went well beyond religious liberty, resting instead on a citizen's right to freedom of conscience. Indeed, one even has the right to refuse to express a commitment to liberty itself. In 1977, the United States Supreme Court, in the case of *Wooley v. Maynard*, ruled that the state of New Hampshire could not require its residents to display the state's "Live Free or Die" motto if they disagreed with its message. As plaintiff George Maynard wrote to the court, "I believe that life is more precious than freedom." The import of the court's ruling is that the state does not have the right to force anyone to voice an idea he or she is opposed to, even if that idea is liberty itself.

This approach is at the center of a crucial Supreme Court decision. The Court, of course, reviews cases already decided by lower courts. Normally, when the Court chooses to hear a case, it calls for a full hearing, with new legal briefs and with oral arguments, after which it writes its own opinion. In this case, however, the Court apparently believed the principle at stake in the case to be so clear, and the lower court's decision on the issue so obviously correct, that it did not see a need to hear new arguments or to offer its own analysis. Instead, it simply approved what the lower court did and said. That is a powerful affirmation, and the case is important enough to merit some extensive discussion.

In 1985, Judge Frank Easterbrook, of the United States Court of Appeals for the Seventh Circuit, which is just below the Supreme Court in authority, wrote the appellate court's opinion in the crucial case of *American Booksellers Association Inc. v. Hudnut*. The city of Indianapolis had enacted and enforced an antipornography ordinance that claimed to protect women from "subordination." Judge Easterbrook saw through the ordinance's disguise as a "civil rights" law and described it as an effort to coerce a change in attitudes. Noting that supporters of the ordinance "say that it will play an important role in reducing the tendency of men to view women as sexual objects," he concluded that it faced an insurmountable constitutional obstacle: It not only sought to alter *attitudes* (which is bad enough), but it did so in a manner that discriminated by *viewpoint*. The law favored, he correctly noted, only "speech treating women in the approved way—in sexual encounters 'premised on equality.'" The First Amendment, he ruled, prohibits the state both from establishing a "preferred viewpoint" for or about a group, and from taking steps to change private attitudes to suit such an ideological preference.

In language that seems directly to address the academics and administrators who draft mandatory campus sensitivity training programs and ideologically biased freshmen orientations, the court concluded that a free society protects the right of individuals to choose, freely and for themselves, those things that affect "how people see the world, their fellows, and social relations." Responding to the city's argument that pornography poisoned the atmosphere for women, the judge rejected any "answer [that] leaves the government in control of all of the institutions of culture, the great censor and director of which thoughts are good for us." The First Amendment, Judge Easterbrook and his colleagues ruled, permitted neither "thought control" nor an officially "approved view of women, of how they may react to sexual encounters [and] of how the sexes may relate to each other."

The city appealed to the Supreme Court, challenging the Circuit Court's ruling that Indianapolis's antipornography "civil rights" ordinance was unconstitutional. The Supreme Court, after accepting the case for review, found the issues so clear that it affirmed Judge Easterbook's judgment summarily—that is, without even calling for further argument. In short, the decision of the Court of Appeals now has the binding and official force of the United States Supreme Court. It is the law of the land. Under the First Amendment, clearly, there can be no "approved view of women" and of "how the sexes may relate to each other." There can be no imposition of regimes aimed at changing the attitudes of free citizens by coercion. Freedom of conscience, in America, is an essential legal and moral value, and it begins with the recognition that we are a nation of free individuals who may define for ourselves the deepest part of our being.

This does not mean, of course, that there can be no laws banning true discriminatory *practices*. However, the First Amendment draws a line between laws that control one's *actions* and laws that seek to control one's speech or, more profoundly still, one *beliefs and attitudes*.

FREEDOM OF CONSCIENCE: A RIGHT FOR BOTH THE RELIGIOUS AND THE SECULAR

Many wrongly believe that freedom of conscience refers only to religious conscience. Such a restriction, of course, itself would constitute viewpoint discrimination. In fact, someone's objection to campus "thought control" need not be rooted in religion in order to be constitutionally protected. This area of law has not been fully explored by the courts, but there seems to be no constitutional rule or doctrine limiting protection to *religiously* based objections to, say, diversity training, but not granting protection to those with *philosophical* or *ethical* objections. *Barnette* specifically concluded, it is worth repeating, "If there is any fixed star in our constitutional constellation, it is that no official, high or petty, can prescribe what shall be orthodox *in politics, nationalism, religion, or other matters of opinion or force citizens to confess by word or act* their faith" in it. (Emphasis added.)

College administrators at public colleges and universities are the ideal example of the "petty" officials to whom *Barnette* applies.

The Supreme Court followed such an expansive approach in interpreting a federal law that exempted religious objectors from the military draft. In *U.S. v. Seeger* (1965), the Court stated that "A sincere and meaningful belief which occupies in the life of its possessor a place parallel to that filled by the God of those admittedly qualifying for the exemption comes within the statutory definition." Thus, to the extent that the law gives an advantage to a person because of his or her religious belief (in this instance, the privilege of not engaging in war based upon a religiously based conscientious objection) the state must accord the same privilege to a person whose philosophical views are comparable in intensity and personal significance to a religious belief. Applied to the issue of thought reform, this principle suggests that the government (including state colleges and universities) may not seek to force a person to adopt a belief that violates either his or her religious or deeply held philosophical values.

THE CONSTITUTIONALLY PROTECTED RIGHT TO CONSCIENCE

The authors of the First Amendment understood full well that people with power have a dark tendency to abuse it, to use coercion, and to suppress competing ideas. With great foresight, the framers erected specific provisions in the First Amendment to prevent such abuses, protecting an individual's right to hold his or her own opinions, to speak or publish them freely in the marketplace of ideas, to join with other like-minded individuals to promote their common viewpoints, and to practice his or her religion without interference from the state. These First Amendment rights, taken together, protect an individual's right to believe, or, in other words, the right to conscience.

Students in today's universities must remember that the Constitution protects their right to freedom of conscience and belief at public universities, and that many private colleges guarantee such freedoms by their own stated policies, procedures and, indeed, promises and assurances. Students should understand and know why it is important to protect their right to freedom of conscience against such ideological coercion from those in power.

THE RIGHT TO BELIEVE

The freedom to believe, or the right of conscience, is the foundation of all other First Amendment rights. The Supreme Court views the right of conscience as so fundamental that *no* state interest can justify an infringement upon it. (In contrast, speech may be curtailed in the face of a demonstrated "compelling" state interest, and, further, speech is subject to reasonable restrictions in terms of the time, place, and manner in which the speech is delivered. (See *FIRE's Guide to Free Speech on Campus* for an explanation of these limitations.) This view of the essential nature and broad scope of the right of conscience has been articulated in a long series of Supreme Court opinions.

In 1878, in a case rejecting the argument by Mormon polygamists that their right to free exercise of religion exempted them from criminal prosecution for bigamy, the Supreme Court ruled that the government may not prosecute people for holding disfavored *beliefs*, but can prosecute them for illegal *actions*. The Court put it this way: "Laws are made for the government of actions, and while they cannot interfere with mere religious beliefs and opinions, they may with practices" (*Reynolds v. U.S.* [1878]). The Supreme Court has reaffirmed this principle that beliefs are absolutely protected from governmental interference in such important cases as *Cantwell v. Connecticut* (1940) and *Bowen v. Roy* (1986).

For many, as noted, the Supreme Court's most important and comprehensive right of conscience case is the 1943 decision of *West Virginia State Board of Education v. Barnette*, discussed earlier in some detail. What is crucial about *Barnette* is that the Court chose not to decide the case solely on the basis of the religious liberty clauses of the First Amendment (the salute to the flag, recall, was seen by Jehovah's Witnesses as contrary to Biblical teachings against idolatry). Instead, the Court's opinion protected, in broad terms, the freedom not to believe in, or even mouth agreement with, secular and religious orthodoxies approved by those who happen to be in power at any given time.

What is certain is that a state college or university may not infringe on a student's right to believe. However, courts have had few opportunities to rule on precisely how and in what contexts state school officials must respect an individual's right to believe. University officials would undoubtedly argue that the entire point of a college experience is *education*, being exposed to differing viewpoints, having one's own beliefs challenged so that they are either strengthened or discarded in the crucible of open debate. They would therefore argue that it's perfectly acceptable to force students to be exposed even to views or to an experience or belief that some would consider wicked or harmful.

Although there is a good measure of truth in such an argument, the First Amendment does place limits on what a state university can do to advance learning or to further a student's education. For example, no educational or pedagogical reason would justify a government school forcing students to attend mandatory chapel services, to recite the Pledge of Allegiance, or to pledge to adhere to certain beliefs as a condition of attending or graduating from that school. Such enforced ideological activity or belief quite clearly crosses a line between true education and what might otherwise be deemed "brainwashing," "thought reform," or, the older term, "indoctrination."

Of course, it would be perfectly acceptable for a professor to require students to *study* and even to *memorize* passages from religious documents, the *Communist Manifesto*, or any other ideologically charged materials, but only if it is part of a genuine educational program in which the students are not required to make statements of belief in or agreement with those materials. While the line between education and coerced ideological conformity is sometimes difficult to decide in close cases, a careful reading of some of the leading Supreme Court cases (especially *Barnette*) can usually help the analysis.

PRINCIPLES OF ACADEMIC FREEDOM: AMERICAN ASSOCIATION OF UNIVERSITY PROFESSORS

The American Association of University Professors (AAUP) has provided the most authoritative and widely accepted definition of academic freedom in the United States. After having been enlisted to help resolve several high-profile disputes between university administrators and individual professors, the AAUP, in 1915, appointed a committee that drafted guidelines that would define more concretely the views widely accepted in the United States and parts of Europe, but which had proven difficult to specify and implement. The resulting document (the *General Report of the Committee on Academic Freedom and Tenure*) was heavily influenced by the idea that truth was not a fixed absolute, but, rather, a goal continually pursued in a university in which individuals had the "complete and unlimited freedom to pursue inquiry and publish its results." The 1915 report was less intent on giving specific rights to professors than on ensuring that the pursuit of knowledge and truth by the faculty in general would proceed unhindered by any authority or force. The university was to be a refuge from *all* tyrannies over men's minds—whether exercised by the state, the university trustees, or by public opinion.

The report, in addition to recognizing professors' freedom of unfettered inquiry, also recognized their freedom to teach their particular fields without interference as to content, except when the execution of their teaching duties could fairly be classified as incompetent or neglectful.

There was, however, a notable exception to the professor's freedom to teach whatever he, in his sound professional judgment, wished when dealing with young students. The teacher was admonished to avoid "taking unfair advantage of the student's immaturity by indoctrinating him with the teacher's own opinions before the student has had an opportunity fairly to examine other opinions upon the matters in question, and before he has sufficient knowledge and ripeness of judgment to be entitled to form any definitive opinion of his own."

The 1915 AAUP document was updated and expanded in 1940, and again in 1967. In its *Joint Statement on Rights and Freedoms of Students* (1967), the AAUP addressed the principle of academic freedom as it relates to students: "Students should be encouraged to develop the capacity for critical judgment and to engage in a sustained and independent search for truth.... [They] should be free to take reasoned exception to the data or views offered in any course of study and to reserve judgment about matters of opinion." *The Joint Statement* also noted that "students should have protection through orderly procedures against prejudiced or capricious academic evaluation." In 2000, the AAUP reaffirmed the necessity of these fundamental rights in its *Statement on Graduate Students:* "Graduate programs in universities exist for the discovery and transmission of knowledge, the education of students, the training of future faculty, and the general well-being of society. Free inquiry and free expression are indispensable to the attainment of these goals."

When a court intervenes in a university's refusal to extend free speech rights to a student, it does so under the legal rubric of enforcing a constitutional or statutory right to free speech rather than enforcing a precept of academic freedom. Courts, after all, interpret and enforce constitutions and statutes, not AAUP policies, unless a professor or student sues the university for a breach of a contract that promised academic freedom. Nonetheless, the concepts of free speech and academic freedom have become intertwined. Courts, in fact, as part of the judicial enforcement of constitutional rights, have come to enforce certain principles of academic freedom as defined by the academic profession. In 1967, in the landmark case of *Keyeshian v. Board of Regents of the*

University of the State of New York, the Supreme Court held that "our Nation is deeply committed to safeguarding academic freedom, [a] transcendent value to all of us and not merely to the teachers concerned." The Court found that the First Amendment "does not tolerate laws that cast a pall of orthodoxy over the classroom...[which is] peculiarly the marketplace of ideas."

CAMPUS THOUGHT REFORM: DIVERSITY TRAINING AND ORIENTATION PROGRAMS

Some colleges and universities openly communicate that they operate from a specific set of ideas as essential truths and expressly limit opposing ideas on campus: Conservative religious colleges come to mind, along with military academies. There is nothing wrong, or unconstitutional, with this phenomenon of institutions that operate under a prescribed doctrine, ideology, or discipline. This is because these schools openly proclaim their specific mission. Students who consider enrolling at such schools have clear notice, warning, and under-standing of what kind of school they will be attending and what they should expect if they express certain dis-senting views. The Constitution permits private schools to promote their own beliefs, because the Constitution protects the right of free association, the right of people to join together with like-minded people to advance a common set of ideals. Indeed, such institutions contribute to American pluralism and diversity or choice. What the Constitution *prohibits* is the *state* coercing the minds of those who dissent from a state dogma.

The problem—and the conflict with the principles that inform the First Amendment as well as with principles of academic freedom—is with those colleges and universities that claim to welcome debate and dissent, but then impose a secular orthodoxy on their students. One of the main tools they use to accomplish that goal is mandatory "diversity training" for students.

Alan Charles Kors, a professor at the University of Pennsylvania, coauthor of *The Shadow University: The Betrayal of Liberty on America's Campuses*, and a cofounder of FIRE, wrote of the "Orwellian implications of today's college orientation" programs in his article, "Thought Reform 101," published in *Reason* (March 2000) and available on the FIRE website (www.thefire.org). He examines several diversity training programs at various colleges and universities, exposing how each of them violates the rights of conscience and belief, and concludes: "The assault on individual identity was essential to the horror and inhumanity of Jim Crow laws, of apartheid, and of the Nuremburg Race Laws. It is no less inhuman when undertaken by 'diversity educators.'"

In particular, Kors focuses on *Blue Eyed*, a "two-and-a-half-hour exercise in sadism," in which trainer Jane Elliott "divides her group into stupid, lazy, shiftless, incompetent, and psychologically brutalized 'blue eyes,' on the one hand, and clever and empowered 'brown eyes,' on the other." In the words of her own publicity materials, Elliott "does not intellectualize highly emotionally charged or challenging topics...She uses participants' own emotions to make them feel discomfort, guilt, shame, embarrassment, and humiliation." Kors sees this as appallingly similar to the brainwashing described in George Orwell's *1984*: "In *Blue Eyed*, the facilitator, Jane Elliott, says of those under her authority for the day, 'A new reality is going to be created for these people.' She informs everyone of the rules of the event: 'You have no power, absolutely no power.' By the end, broken and in tears, they see their own racist evil, and they love Big Sister."

Diversity training that seeks to indoctrinate students—intrusively and without the right to question, dissent, and debate—about the supposedly false nature of their beliefs and about the need to change may very well cross the line between education and violation of the constitutional right of conscience. State colleges and universities should allow students who object to such programs the right to opt out of such training sessions or else restructure the events to ensure that students are free to disagree with the viewpoints expressed in sensitivity training. (Thoughtful debates among conflicting viewpoints would be yet better and closer to the spirit of education.) While the very notion of "training" (as distinguished from "education") is antithetical to both liberty and dignity, an opt-out would take some of the edge from such programs. The state still plays the improper role of "Big Teacher," but at least the student is allowed to avoid the indoctrination and therefore cannot claim a personal injury. Note that in the *Barnette* case the Jehovah's Witness students did not eliminate the Pledge to the Flag being said in the public school classes—and, indeed, they did not even try to do so—but simply got the right to stand silent and opt out of pledging. Of course, the Pledge is not quite the same as "diversity training," since the Supreme Court specifically said that inculcating patriotic values was a reasonable undertaking for a public elementary school, warning, however, against the creation of a state "orthodoxy" on such matters. It is clear, by contrast, that state universities should not seek to "train" adult students to hold certain social and political views.

THE RIGHT OF
ASSOCIATION AND
MANDATORY DIVERSITY
TRAINING FOR STUDENTS

Mandatory diversity training, in its more extreme forms, as it is done on many campuses today, likely infringes unconstitutionally on a student's individual right to believe. Less extreme versions of diversity training may pass constitutional muster, but they should still raise concerns about freedom of conscience.

There has not yet been a direct challenge in a federal court to a mandatory diversity training program on a public college campus. However, there is good reason to believe that the more intrusive of these programs would be ruled unconstitutional. The two critical factors that raise constitutional questions about a diversity training program are (1) required attendance and (2) the goal of changing the individual students' fundamental beliefs to a preapproved set of beliefs, by methods that make clear to the students that, in certain areas of ideology and belief, dissent or deviance is not acceptable.

The government may announce its own message in the marketplace of ideas, urging people to stop smoking or to buy United States Savings Bonds. People who disagree or decide they just don't want to hear the government's message may take steps to avoid hearing it and certainly are not required to indicate their agreement in terms of their voiced opinions or, most of the time, even their conduct.

When a state university forces people to hear its message by imposing it on a captive audience, however, the requirement to sit and listen to a political and social orthodoxy itself raises constitutional concerns. Mandatory attendance requirements at such an event indicate a constitutional violation of the attending students' rights, forcing unwilling students to listen to a presentation that they would not attend absent the compulsion. This is especially true when the compulsion aims at changing and imposing beliefs. (Unlike a mandatory session of *Blue Eyed*, for example, a required introductory course in World History is governed by all of the rules of academic freedom and of a student's right to dissent and disagree.)

A state university cannot justify coercive forms of mandatory diversity training on the grounds that someone can simply go to school somewhere else. This would not justify mandatory religious chapel services at a state university, and it does not justify diversity training intended to change a student's beliefs.

Of course, the Constitution protects a person's (such as a professor's) right to *persuade* someone to adopt his or her viewpoint, even when the persuasion is forceful and passionate. The government crosses a line when it forces students to attend and to listen to presentations intended to change their beliefs, and then either requires them to voice agreement or forbids them to disagree openly. Mandatory diversity training is likely unconstitutional if it is presented in an environment where students are not allowed to question the presentation of the "orthodox," official view, where they are not allowed to debate or voice opposing views to the government's views, and where the state sets up the diversity training in a way that requires or strongly pressures students to conform or be silent. In a sense, the line between permissible education and unconstitutional "training" is demonstrated by the very use of the word "training," which implies coercion rather than intellectual choice. One doesn't "train" a pet by intellectual persuasion.

It is not necessarily an adequate defense for the state school to claim that students only have to sit through the presentation and do not have to believe what they hear. The government of West Virginia did not require the students in the *Barnette* case, who were Jehovah's Witnesses, to believe the words of the Pledge of Allegiance; all that was required was that the students pledge to the flag. The Supreme Court ruled precisely that forced participation in that patriotic ceremony went beyond the state's legitimate powers. Although many presentations and lectures will pass constitutional muster as long as the student is permitted to remain silent (for instance, it is not a constitutional violation if those students who object sit in silence while the rest of the room recites the Pledge of Allegiance), an exceptionally heavy-handed ceremony in which one's mere presence implies belief is probably unconstitutional. (For example, for many religious students, their required presence at religious services of another religion or denomination, even if they are not forced to pray, would violate their religious consciences.)

Courts have not decided precisely what kinds of state programs or exercises violate a student's right of conscience by officially trying to change his or her chosen system of belief. This is a largely unexplored area of law. Nonetheless, there are examples of threats to the right of conscience that would stand a very good chance of being declared unconstitutional if challenged. Examples might be: When a campus official requires students to say a "diversity pledge"; when a campus official pressures students to "show support for the troops" by supporting United States foreign policy; when a campus diversity trainer tells an 18-year-old rural freshman that she must eradicate latent racism or heterosexism from her attitudes; when a student judicial affairs official tells a

Muslim student that his religious beliefs must be changed because they promote subjugation of women; or, indeed, when officials force students to take part in exercises where students must reveal their inner thoughts and moral beliefs before a group of scrutinizing peers, pressuring the student to conform. Identifying students who hold the "wrong" beliefs and subjecting them to techniques to purge them of their ideological errors suggest a gross violation of a student's right to believe.

ACADEMIC DEMANDS FOR
IDEOLOGICAL UNIFORMITY

Other ways that supposedly tolerant campuses suppress the freedom of conscience and the freedom to believe include limitations on classroom discussions. The faculty of St. Cloud State's Department of Social Work in Minnesota announced that students could not major in social work if they hold the point of view, regarding homosexuality, that one may "hate the sin and love the sinner." Such a theological view would make them incapable of dealing with homosexuals, the faculty members decided. In doing so, St. Cloud had decided that certain devout people of faith are incapable of benefiting society as social workers unless they renounce and change their deeply held beliefs.

At Citrus College in Glendora, California, a professor teaching a required course in speech compelled undergraduate students to write antiwar letters to President

George W. Bush. To receive the maximum score in the course, students had to write letters to President Bush "demanding" that he not go to war with Iraq. Students who asked to write letters supporting the president were told that this would be unacceptable and that they would not receive extra credit.

At Rhode Island College, the Poverty Institute (a school of social work) required its students to lobby the state legislature—and advocate school-approved positions—regardless of the student's own beliefs. Further, a faculty member responded to a student who challenged the perceived ideological bias of his teachers by telling him that he should perhaps consider another area of study if he did not agree with the ideology of the department.

A Columbia University professor refused to permit a student to dissent from his characterization of Israeli actions during the Israeli army's battle against Palestinian militants in the Jenin refugee camp. Declaring that he would not permit anyone in his classroom to "deny" evidence of "Israeli atrocities," the professor shut down discussion in class and violated that student's academic freedom.

By limiting classroom discussion and silencing dissent, professors violate the rights of conscience of their students. The clear aim is not merely to advocate a point of view but to coerce, if necessary, their students into believing the professor's or school's version of truth. Such oppressive actions clearly cross the line between education and indoctrination.

PROFESSORS' POLICIES LIMITING CLASSROOM DISCUSSION

Professors violate students' right to believe if they require them to assent to a set of beliefs before they can enter into class discussions. A professor may have ground rules to ensure civility and order, and a professor should insist upon mastery of a subject (while protecting a student's right to reasoned dissent), but a professor has no right to demand ideological uniformity. Similarly, a state school may not constitutionally require students to hold a certain belief in order to complete a specific college major. A student in a political science class may not be required to state approval of the president's military policies. A theology major cannot be required to renounce her atheism, or a social work major to renounce his opposition to legal recognition of nontraditional families, or a labor history major to renounce her allegiance to the free enterprise system or her admiration of

Marxism. That is not to say, of course, that requiring students to work with certain basic assumptions of the discipline, without being forced to voice a true belief in them, would violate their rights to conscience. A "young Earth" Christian fundamentalist (*i.e.*, one who believes, based on Biblical genealogies, that the Earth is 6,000 years old) cannot learn modern geology unless she is willing temporarily or conditionally or at least hypothetically to set aside or compartmentalize her "young Earth" beliefs in order to learn mainstream geological theories. An ardent Communist cannot learn mainstream economics if he is not willing temporarily to set aside or compartmentalize his own beliefs when learning about free market economic theories that are founded on assumptions that contradict his own ideology. What crosses the line is when the Christian fundamentalist or the Communist, despite learning the discipline and meeting all of its academic requirements, is denied his or her degree or given a lower grade purely for refusing to believe or mouth support for the tenets of the discipline that he or she has mastered.

Examples of classroom requirements that cross this line come from the University of South Carolina and the University of Southern California, among many others, where professors required students to agree to a set of viewpoints before they could enter into classroom discussions. At the University of Southern California, students had to "acknowledge that racism, classism, sexism, heterosexism, and other institutionalized forms of oppression exist" as a precondition for enrolling in one professor's class. Students also had to "agree to combat actively the myths and stereotypes about our own groups and other groups so that we can break down the walls that prohibit group cooperation and group gain." In a class at the University of South Carolina, students had to agree that "everyone [in the world] does his or her best." The words "acknowledge" and "agree" are clear signs of coercion.

Universities that claim to inculcate and encourage independent, critical, and inquiring minds in students cannot turn around and force students to conform to a set of ideas, or to suffer for expressing views deviating from the party line. In higher education, there is no official orthodoxy to which a student may be forced to voice his or her agreement.

IDEOLOGICAL REQUIREMENTS FOR STUDENT GROUP RECOGNITION

Many universities require all campus organizations to sign nondiscrimination statements in order to meet on campus and to gain official recognition by the school. While it is a good thing, in fact, that the chess team, for example, cannot exclude members by race or national origin, campus administrators are increasingly using the nondiscrimination statements as weapons to try to drive certain disfavored student groups off campus.

Rutgers and the University of North Carolina-Chapel Hill attempted to ban Inter-Varsity Christian Fellowship chapters from their campuses because this Christian organization required its leaders to be Christian and to profess adherence to fundamental Christian beliefs. The chapters claimed that their whole purpose was for like-minded students to promote their Christian beliefs, so to allow an atheist or some adherent of a non-Christian religion, or even a Christian who refuses to accept certain fundamental tenets, to lead their group would undermine their entire reason for being. Both universities backed down or at least compromised in the face of withering criticism from inside and outside the university. Just as the campus Gay, Lesbian, Bisexual, and Transgendered organization has a right to organize around expanding the rights of and respect for its members and their ways of life, so do students of faith have a right to organize about their common beliefs and purposes.

Other campuses punished student groups for holding the "wrong" views, or at least officially disapproved views. Tufts University attempted to exile a student Christian group from campus by withdrawing official recognition because the group enforced its views on "traditional marriage" by refusing to permit a lesbian who disagreed with the group's position to seek selection as its leader. (Homosexuals were allowed to be *members* of the group, but were disqualified from being *leaders* if they took the position that participating in a homosexual activity was not sinful.)

The student government of the Washington University School of Law in St. Louis, Missouri refused to recognize a student pro-life group because student government leaders decided that the group was inadequately "pro-life." The student government decided that the group needed to oppose the death penalty in order to have a consistent pro-life philosophy and not just advocate "pro-life principles as applied to abortion, euthanasia, and assisted suicide" as the student group had originally intended. When the student governmental entity told a private organization what beliefs it had to espouse, Washington University School of Law triggered a firestorm of protest, including criticism from liberal editorial pages and from the ACLU. The student government changed its mind and allowed the student group to meet on campus and to determine for itself what beliefs it would espouse.

Although this particular abuse of antidiscrimination regulations has at present been applied most commonly to conservative Christian groups, it could easily be applied to others. What if, for example, a left-wing, pro-Palestinian campus group that permitted only anti-Zionists to join was accused of excluding Jews? These principles protect the right of association for all groups, regardless of the changing winds of campus politics, and people from all ideological points of the compass should cooperate to protect them, even if they bitterly disagree on other issues. Having a great variety of *different* groups, far from reducing diversity, adds greatly, in fact, to campus diversity and pluralism.

SPEECH CODES

One way in which colleges and universities accomplish a selective censorship that invades the individual's conscience is by ideologically biased campus speech or "harassment" codes that seek to enforce a particular point of view or campus orthodoxy. Those codes prevent students from engaging in speech that might offend others on the basis of sex, sexual orientation, race, and similar criteria, on the theory that the civil rights of minority students or women will be enhanced if they are not put into the position of having to hear words and ideas that they might find insulting. Students are expected to adopt the administrator's point of view that it is better to shut up than to express a belief or point of view, even if truly believed and deeply held, that might offend a minority group member. Even if the student does not adopt or agree with the administrator's point of view, however, he is required nonetheless to keep his mouth shut rather than express certain ideas.

These codes are an example of a particularly ideological form of censorship, since, by their very terms, nearly all of them seek to censor speech that might offend members of "historically disadvantaged groups," typically defined by sex, race, ethnicity, or sexual orientation. These speech codes help enforce a particular political and philosophical point of view favored by administrators—that members of such defined groups should be treated unequally. (These codes are discussed in more detail in *FIRE's Guide to Free Speech on Campus*.)

In 2001, the United States Court of Appeals for the Third Circuit declared unconstitutional the harassment policy for the school district located in State College, Pennsylvania. While State College Area School District consists primarily of elementary and grammar schools, the court's decision is highly relevant to college and university students and administrators, because findings of unconstitutional restrictions on younger students apply with yet greater force to university students. That policy barred the following speech:

> Harassment means verbal or physical conduct based on one's actual or perceived race, religion, color, national origin, gender, sexual orientation, disability, or other personal characteristics, and which has the purpose or effect of substantially interfering with a student's educational performance or creating an intimidating, hostile or offensive environment.

The Policy continued by providing several examples of "harassment":

> Harassment can include any unwelcome verbal, written or physical conduct which offends, denigrates or belittles an individual because of any of the characteristics described above. Such conduct includes, but is not limited to, unsolicited derogatory remarks, jokes, demeaning comments or behaviors, slurs, mimicking, name calling, graffiti, innuendo, gestures, physical contact, stalking, threatening, bullying, extorting or the display or circulation of written material or pictures.

The code went so far as to ban "other harassment" on the basis of one's "clothing, physical appearance, social skills, peer group, intellect, educational program, hobbies or values, etc." This ban on "harassing" people on the basis of their values was particularly telling. Personal values are those aspects of conscience that most truly make a human being an individual. To say that one may not criticize others' values is essentially to say that one may not have strongly held values of one's own, or, at the very least, that one must not mention those values when disagreeing with someone else.

In *Saxe v. State College Area School District* (2001), the United States Court of Appeals, quoting from several United States Supreme Court decisions, wrote the following about these extraordinary provisions:

> [A]ttempting to proscribe negative comments about "values," as that term is commonly used today, is something else alto-

gether. By prohibiting disparaging speech directed at a person's "values," the Policy strikes at the heart of moral and political discourse—the lifeblood of constitutional self-government (and democratic education) and the core concern of the First Amendment. That speech about "values" may offend is not cause for its prohibition, but rather the reason for its protection: "a principal 'function of free speech under our system of government is to invite dispute. It may indeed best serve its high purpose when it induces a condition of unrest, creates dissatisfaction with conditions as they are, or even stirs people to anger...'" No court or legislature has ever suggested that unwelcome speech directed at another's "values" may be prohibited under the rubric of anti-discrimination.

The Court of Appeals struck down the policy as "overbroad," that is, it banned too much speech that is protected under the First Amendment, rather than only focusing on unprotected expression. For example, "derogatory remarks, jokes, demeaning comments, slurs, mimicking, innuendo," and so on all could be protected speech advocating controversial views, (e.g., "I think all Christians are hypocrites"; "Saddam should have gassed all American invaders"; "One day, a priest, a rabbi and a lesbian went fishing"; and so on.)

Of course, a college can ban true harassment, but it must carefully draw the lines of its policy only to ban harassing conduct and not pure expression. As the federal Court of Appeals said in *Saxe*:

> There is of course no question that non-expressive, physically harassing *conduct* is entirely outside the ambit of the

free speech clause. But there is also no question that the free speech clause protects a wide variety of speech that listeners may consider deeply offensive, including statements that impugn another's race or national origin or that denigrate religious beliefs.

A college does not convert protected *speech* into unprotected *conduct* by calling disfavored speech a "verbal act" or "harassment."

As the Court of Appeals in *Saxe* summarized various Supreme Court cases:

> The Supreme Court has held time and again, both within and outside of the school context, that the mere fact that someone might take offense at the content of speech is not sufficient justification for prohibiting it.

Therefore, students who are threatened by university officials with punishment for violating a "speech code" might wish to contact a lawyer to determine whether the policy violates the Constitution's protection for freedom of speech. (They also might wish to contact FIRE.)

MANDATORY
PSYCHOLOGICAL
COUNSELING

A fairly recent and profoundly disturbing trend is the use of mandatory "psychological counseling" as a tool of the judicial affairs office. Students found guilty of wrongs that involve "hateful" or "antisocial" behavior may be required to see a psychologist, or, indeed, a specific social worker, before returning to school. In this way, a violation of a code or rule banning speech that might be perceived as insulting or otherwise unpleasant by members of what are deemed "historically disadvantaged groups" is classified instead as a symptom of a psychological problem on the part of the student.

To designate deviations from campus orthodoxy as somehow pathological is another way of elevating the notion of "political correctness" to the highest moral plane, or, indeed, to the level of psychological health. This technique is not unheard of in totalitarian societies. The former Soviet Union, for example, was infamous for placing political dissidents in psychiatric hospitals, on the theory that disagreement with the State or the Party constituted a sign of mental illness.

Mandatory psychological counseling can take many forms. Sometimes it does not even involve a trained psychologist or psychiatrist, but rather a series of meetings with an administrator, or the director of the Women's Center, or even a clergyman. Students sometimes accept such "treatment" as an alternative to a harsh penalty, even if they do not believe they are mentally ill or psychologically unbalanced.

It is, of course, up to each individual student charged with a "hate speech" offense to decide whether to defend himself or herself on grounds of principle such as are set forth in this *Guide*, or to accept the compromise of being labeled "troubled" and given "treatment" in order to cure "antisocial tendencies." The decision as to how to proceed, given such a choice, will depend upon the particular student's confidence in his or her ability (and willingness) to fight to the bitter end, versus a desire to "put it behind " and avoid the possibility of a disciplinary record. (Frequently, when the student opts for counseling rather than a disciplinary hearing or trial, the school will agree not to place the counseling on the student's permanent record, an effort by the school to avoid a show-down with the student whose only offense consists of uttering words and ideas the courts would recognize as constitutionally protected.)

QUESTIONS AND ANSWERS

I am a freshman at a state university. During orientation, we were required to take diversity training. The diversity trainer told us that we were all racist, sexist homophobes who benefited from "white privilege." She derided us as naive and blind to our own latent prejudice. She pressured us to reveal personal details about our beliefs and private activities to a group of peers I had met only the day before. I felt very uncomfortable. Does the law allow me to be excused from such sessions?

This is an area of the law where we do not have any direct, definitive, and authoritative court rulings. Nonetheless, the Supreme Court has stated that the Constitution strongly protects the right of conscience, sometimes called the right to believe or not believe. If the point of the training is to coerce you to change your beliefs, then the training raises important constitutional questions concerning the right to conscience.

In addition, any such requirement that a student disclose personal beliefs or intimate details about himself or herself runs afoul of another constitutional protection that is tangential to the right to conscience on which this *Guide* focuses, namely, the right to privacy. Just as the state does not have the right to impose beliefs on a person, so it does not have the right to delve into a person's mind in order to see what is there. In this regard, the reader would do well to read the opinion of the Supreme Court in the 1969 case of *Stanley v. Georgia* which, while upholding state laws against the production and distribution of obscene materials, barred states from prosecuting the mere private *possession* of such materials at home. In establishing "conditions favorable to the pursuit of happiness," Justice Thurgood Marshall wrote for the majority, the drafters of the Constitution "recognized the significance of man's spiritual nature, of his feelings and of his intellect." The quintessentially human realm of private intellect, whether base or sublime, was beyond the control of the state: "Our whole constitutional heritage rebels at the thought of giving government the power to control men's minds."

This type of training becomes more constitutionally questionable when it is mandatory. The university must, at the very least, allow students who find such training objectionable to opt out or to walk out of it when it becomes indecently intrusive. A university administration that is wise and that takes its educational task seriously will avoid altogether such "training" of students' minds. It is fine if students graduate while holding beliefs that are different from the administration's "official line" as to what is "correct" and what is "incorrect." Again as the Supreme Court observed in *Barnette*, "compulsory unification of opinion achieves only the unanimity of the graveyard," and we must preserve "intellectual individualism," "rich cultural diversities," and the "right to differ as to things that touch the heart of the existing order."

One occasional activity used in such sessions is for the diversity trainer to instruct students to line up in order of skin color and hue (lightest to darkest, or *vice versa*) and then to comment on the feeling and social meaning of their respective positions in the line. The degree of ideological coercion, and hence the constitutionality, of the activity depends on what comments are allowed or prohibited. If, for instance, students must explain their position in the "color line" solely in terms of structural racism or white privilege, then the activity has probably crossed the line into unconstitutional ideological coercion. If, however, students are permitted (or, better, encouraged) to question the purpose of the line-up, the sanity of the organizers, and the underlying assumptions of the activity, then the session is more likely to pass constitutional muster.

Another common activity is for the diversity trainer to instruct students to sort themselves into groups defined by race, sex, or sexual orientation. (Regardless of its constitutionality, the wisdom of instructing students who are fresh out of high school to "out" themselves as gay, lesbian, questioning, or whatever else, in front of relative strangers at orientation seems questionable at best.) Those who sort themselves into the "privileged" groups (*e.g.*, white, straight, male) are told to describe the advantages they have benefited from as privileged, while those in the "oppressed" groups (*e.g.*, racial minorities, gays, and women) are told to describe how they have been harmed by their membership in those groups. The structure of the activity makes it virtually impossible for students to dissent from the political arguments implied by the questions. Because of this, the activity raises serious issues of ideological coercion, as well as invasion of privacy.

Finally, whatever the constitutional issues, these programs are degrading, intellectually insulting, patronizing, divisive, and an arrogant abuse of power. Universities will be hard-pressed to defend such practices if students expose them to the public and the media. Remember what Justice Brandeis once said: "Sunlight is the best disinfectant."

The University's job is educating students. If the University decides to educate students using diver-

sity training, why should a court second-guess the educational experts?

State colleges and universities cannot justify any and all curricular decisions by invoking their educational expertise, and diversity training is almost never given for credit as a formal class governed by the rules of academic freedom. Of course, courts should and do defer to the judgments of school officials in most educational questions, but a state university cannot mandate attendance at chapel services, or require students to recite the Pledge of Allegiance even with the best educational reasons backing up such requirements. Where a legitimate educational decision ends and a constitutional violation begins is not always clear, but such a distinction does exist. It is the court's job to determine when and where that line has been crossed.

Just because an activity is billed as "diversity training" or is politically charged doesn't mean that it contains coercive elements that would implicate the constitutional right to freedom of conscience. For example, a diversity training session that consisted solely of a school official describing the school's speech and harassment policies would not violate freedom of conscience, even if the speech policy itself is constitutionally suspect, because mere presentation of information on the policy does not attempt to coerce *belief* in or *agreement* with the policy. Also, it is not intrusive. Similarly, an ethnic studies course examining the concepts of "internalized oppression" and "structural racism" would not violate freedom of conscience as long as the professor *educated* students and allowed them to reach their own conclusions, rather than *coerced* them to adopt one point of view. Whether the professor makes his or her point of view clear is not relevant; there is no element of coercion unless the professor tries to silence or suppress dissenting opinions.

The professor of my sociology class is a Marxist who derides capitalism and mocks Republicans and students who belong to fraternities or sororities. Another professor is a libertarian who quotes Ayn Rand and speaks contemptuously of socialists and liberals. Students are irritated about the belittling of their respective beliefs. Can these students take any action against these professors?

Probably not, and it's a good thing, too. The professors are not violating the constitutional rights of students by criticizing, even belittling their beliefs. Freewheeling debate is what the First Amendment is meant to protect. Even though a power imbalance exists in a classroom where a professor openly mocks or criticizes students, this is the rough and tumble of a free society. (This is not to say that it is necessarily good pedagogy for a professor to belittle an opposing point of view rather than respond to it with intelligent contrary arguments. However, good versus bad pedagogy is a subject beyond the scope of this *Guide*.) The professor may cross into unconstitutional behavior if, however, he or she repeatedly singles out one student for personal derision and humiliation or for lower grades because of the beliefs the student holds. Professors may not insist that students profess belief in a certain viewpoint, as the college professor did who required her students to write President George W. Bush to criticize the war in Iraq. Professors do have academic freedom, but, as state actors, they too may be found to have violated a student's right to conscience.

In a mandatory class for my major, the professor hands out "Classroom Discussion Standards" on the first day of class. I must sign a statement saying that I agree to affirm each individual's self worth, will not engage in inappropriate remarks that demean others, acknowledge that I am an unwitting recipient and advocate of a white male Eurocentric patriarchal power structure, and agree to work for structural change that will benefit all peoples, especially people of color and sexual minorities. Can a professor do that?
Although there are not yet any major court opinions directly on this question, it is likely that such standards violate the constitutional rights of college and university students. Professors cannot require students to agree to specific viewpoints or to vague standards of civility that may be easily broken depending on who is interpreting

what they mean. Even at private universities the AAUP guidelines, which most colleges and universities claim to accept, prohibit ideological litmus tests for studying a subject. In addition, if professors stifle debate and hinder the viewpoints that students may express, they undermine the entire purpose of a college education. Classroom guidelines that mandate values and commitment to certain schools of thought create a type of ideological loyalty oath that is injurious to intellectual freedom. (If you argue that such a requirement is in fact a type of loyalty oath, such as flourished during the McCarthy period, when individuals were instructed to sign oaths of loyalty to the government of the United States, you might very well cause the professor or administrator to see his or her tyrannical requirements in a light more favorable to you. Most people seeking to impose such requirements do not realize that they are akin to loyalty oaths.) A university in which students are not allowed to disagree with their professors on fundamental assumptions about reality is incapable of intellectual innovation, critical dialogue, meaningful discourse, or true scholarship. Any university that honors academic freedom may not stipulate a commitment to any one political philosophy as a condition of participation in the classroom or tell students what their beliefs must be in order to attain a degree. This is true no matter what the ideology in question. You have recourse to the law, and you have recourse to public exposure of such invasions of your privacy and private beliefs. (You also have recourse to FIRE.)

I am a student desiring to major in social work at my state university. However, the department has a policy that students may not declare a social work major if they hold beliefs that they can "love the sinner but hate the sin" regarding homosexuality. The rationale is that social workers deal with people of varying sexual orientations and that if "judgmental" social workers deep down believe that homosexuality is a sin, they will not interact properly with those they are supposed to serve. May a public college department impose such a requirement?

No. The department is functioning like a "thought police" or "viewpoint police" with such a policy. Students may not be required to affirm or disavow a belief as a requirement to complete a course at the state university. Imagine if you were forbidden from believing deep down that this or that religion were wrong, because you would have to provide services to members of that religion. This restriction violates the Constitution.

My psychology class is requiring me to watch an explicit pornography film as part of the class curriculum. As a Christian, I believe that I can put no unclean thing before my eyes (Psalms 101:3). I cannot sit through a graphic film of sexuality without

defiling myself in violation of my religious beliefs. Does the state university have to grant my request to opt out of watching the film and instead to work on an alternative assignment?

My biology class requires me to dissect fetal pigs. As a Jewish pantheistic pacifist, I cannot do so because my beliefs teach me not to touch dead animals or unclean things or kill things, because they all possess the universal life force. Does the state university have to accommodate my beliefs and allow me an alternative, such as studying a computer program on the internal anatomy of the pig?

Court decisions come down on both sides of whether, or to what extent, the Constitution requires state educational institutions to accommodate the personal or religious beliefs and practices of students. School policies might also guarantee a right for conscientious objectors to opt out of specific assignments. You'll lose, however, if you develop, on the night before the test, a "religious" conviction against taking final exams!

As a matter of constitutional law, the university cannot force you to violate your beliefs. This, however, does not provide you with an absolute right to follow your religious practices in every class you take. In some cases, you may be forced to choose between following your religious practices or taking a particular class. For example, a black nationalist who objects to taking classes with white students, or a white supremacist who objects to taking classes with people of color, would not be able to receive any accommodation for his racially discriminatory beliefs. He would have to choose between learning in an integrated classroom or leaving the integrated class. The proper legal test in such instances is rather complex, and your rights are more fully explained in *FIRE's Guide to Religious Liberty on Campus*.

I belong to a campus Muslim group that has asked its married leader to step down because he said he had become an agnostic and began sleeping with women he met at bars. Our group requires all members to believe in Allah and to refrain from sex outside of marriage. The University is claiming that we have engaged in religious discrimination and marital status discrimination, and is threatening to kick us off campus. May the University do that?
No. The Constitution protects individuals' right to associate with others around common ideas. A state university cannot use its nondiscrimination policies to compel an Islamic group to accept as leaders or members people who do not believe in God and who do not believe or practice the group's standards on sexual activity. The man is free to go start his own "Agnostic Muslims for Sexual Liberty Club" rather than impose his beliefs on others via the school's nondiscrimination policy.

It is important to note, however, that the right to free association does not protect invidious acts of discrimination *unrelated* to the group's purpose. For instance, the chess club would have no right to exclude Catholics, because there is no plausible relationship between being a chess enthusiast and being a non-Catholic. If the chess club were to institute such a restriction, then the university would be acting well within its power in punishing the chess club for religious discrimination. In addition, certain kinds of discrimination have such a long and ugly history that they must be justified by more than a mere rational relationship. Racial discrimination, in particular, is almost never defensible. Any group that bars people from joining based on their race or ethnicity would have an extremely difficult time justifying that policy, even if they argue that the restriction is related to the group's purpose.

CONCLUSION

We hope that this *Guide* makes clear the line over which authority may not step in a quest to mold the minds, beliefs, and consciences of free citizens, including students in a free society. Most people probably think that the world would be a better place if only everyone agreed with them (despite the fact that many such people claim to believe in "diversity"). Many college administrators, alas, act as if they have the power, and even the mission, to mold students' minds to hold "correct" views in certain areas of life. Many of America's laws, doctrines, and values, however, including the First Amendment to the U.S. Constitution and the principles of academic freedom, serve to protect us all from these authoritarian and even totalitarian forces. "Freedom to differ," as the Supreme Court noted of American liberty, "is the right to differ as to things that touch the heart of the existing order." That freedom resides in each human heart and mind. This is the very essence of what it means to be free and human.

FIRE's *GUIDES* TO
STUDENT RIGHTS ON CAMPUS
BOARD OF EDITORS

Vivian Berger – Vivian Berger is the Nash Professor of Law Emerita at Columbia Law School. Berger is a former New York County Assistant District Attorney and a former Assistant Counsel to the NAACP Legal Defense and Educational Fund. She has done significant work in the fields of criminal law and procedure (in particular, the death penalty and habeas corpus) and mediation, and continues to use her expertise in various settings, both public and private. She and her late husband, Professor Curtis J. Berger, are coauthors of "Academic Discipline: A Guide to Fair Process for the University Student," published in the *Columbia Law Review* (volume 99). Berger is General Counsel for and a National Board Member of the American Civil Liberties Union and has written numerous essays and journal articles on human rights and due process.

T. Kenneth Cribb, Jr. – T. Kenneth Cribb, Jr. is the President of the Intercollegiate Studies Institute, a nonpartisan, educational organization dedicated to furthering the American ideal of ordered liberty on college and university campuses. He served as Counselor to the Attorney General of the United States and later as Assistant to the

President for Domestic Affairs during the Reagan administration. Cribb is also President of the Collegiate Network of independent college newspapers. He is former Vice Chairman of the Fulbright Foreign Scholarship Board.

Alan Dershowitz – Alan Dershowitz is the Felix Frankfurter Professor of Law at the Harvard Law School. He is an expert on civil liberties and criminal law and has been described by *Newsweek* as "the nation's most peripatetic civil liberties lawyer and one of its most distinguished defenders of individual rights." Dershowitz is a frequent public commentator on matters of freedom of expression and of due process, and is the author of eighteen books, including, most recently, *Why Terrorism Works: Understanding the Threat, Responding to the Challenge*, and hundreds of magazine and journal articles.

Paul McMasters – Paul McMasters is the First Amendment Ombudsman at the Freedom Forum in Arlington, Virginia. He speaks and writes frequently on all aspects of First Amendment rights, has appeared on various television programs, and has testified before numerous government commissions and congressional committees. Prior to joining the Freedom Forum, McMasters was the Associate Editorial Director of *USA Today*. He is also past National President of the Society of Professional Journalists.

Edwin Meese III – Edwin Meese III holds the Ronald Reagan Chair in Public Policy at the Heritage Foundation. He is also Chairman of Heritage's Center for Legal and Judicial Studies. Meese is a Distinguished Visiting Fellow at the Hoover Institution at Stanford University, and a Distinguished Senior Fellow at The University of London's Institute of United States Studies. He is also Chairman of the governing board at George Mason University in Virginia. Meese served as the 75th Attorney General of the United States under the Reagan administration.

ABOUT FIRE

FIRE's mission is to defend, sustain, and restore individual rights at America's colleges and universities. These rights include freedom of speech, legal equality, due process, religious liberty, and sanctity of conscience—the essential qualities of civil liberty and human dignity. FIRE's core goals are to protect the unprotected against repressive behavior and partisan policies of all kinds, to educate the public about the threat to individual rights that exists on our campuses, and to lead the way in the necessary and moral effort to preserve the rights of students and faculty to speak their minds, to honor their consciences, and to be treated honestly, fairly, and equally by their institutions.

FIRE is a charitable and educational tax-exempt foundation within the meaning of Section 501 (c) (3) of the Internal Revenue Code. Contributions to FIRE are deductible to the fullest extent provided by tax laws. FIRE is funded entirely through individual donations; we receive no government funding. Please visit **www.thefire.org** for more information about FIRE.

FIRE

KNOW YOUR RIGHTS PROGRAM:
FIRE's *GUIDES* TO STUDENT RIGHTS ON CAMPUS PROJECT

FIRE believes it imperative that our nation's future leaders be educated as members of a free society, able to debate and resolve peaceful differences without resort to repression. Toward that end, FIRE implemented its pathbreaking *Guides* to Student Rights on Campus Project.

The creation and distribution of these *Guides* is indispensable to challenging and ending the climate of censorship and enforced self-censorship on our college campuses, a climate profoundly threatening to the future of this nation's full enjoyment of and preservation of liberty. We trust that these *Guides* will enable a wholly new kind of discourse on college and university campuses.

A distinguished group of legal scholars serves as Board of Editors to this series. The board, selected from across the political and ideological spectrum, has advised FIRE on each of the *Guides*. The diversity of this board proves that liberty on campus is not a question of partisan politics, but of the rights and responsibilities of free individuals in a society governed by the rule of law.

It is our liberty, above all else, that defines us as human beings, capable of ethics and responsibility. The struggle for liberty on

American campuses is one of the defining struggles of the age in which we find ourselves. A nation that does not educate in freedom will not survive in freedom and will not even know when it has lost it. Individuals too often convince themselves that they are caught up in moments of history that they cannot affect. That history, however, is made by their will and moral choices. There is a moral crisis in higher education. It will not be resolved unless we choose and act to resolve it. We invite you to join our fight.

Please visit **www.thefireguides.org** for more information on FIRE's *Guides* to Student Rights on Campus.

CONTACTING FIRE
www.thefire.org

Send inquiries, comments, and documented instances of betrayals of free speech, individual liberty, religious freedom, the rights of conscience, legal equality, due process, and academic freedom on campus to:

FIRE's website:
www.thefire.org

By email:
fire@thefire.org

By mail:
601 Walnut Street, Suite 510
Philadelphia, PA 19106

By phone/fax:
215-717-FIRE (3473) (phone)
215-717-3440 (fax)

AUTHORS

Harvey A. Silverglate, is cofounder and a member of the Board of Directors of The Foundation for Individual Rights in Education; coauthor (with Alan Charles Kors) of *The Shadow University: The Betrayal of Liberty on America's Campuses* (The Free Press, 1998; HarperPerennial paperback, 1999); counsel to the Boston law firm of Good & Cormier; the civil liberties columnist for *The Boston Phoenix*; and a contributor of civil liberties columns and writings to a number of regional and national newspapers. He thanks Greg Lukianoff and Carl Takei for their invaluable assistance.

Jordan Lorence is senior counsel for the Alliance Defense Fund, living and working in Phoenix, Arizona. He has litigated First Amendment cases since 1984 in courts across the United States. Mr. Lorence is a graduate of Stanford University and the University of Minnesota Law School. Mr. Lorence argued the *University of Wisconsin v. Southworth* student fees case before the U.S. Supreme Court on behalf of the students in 1999. He has participated as co-counsel in other cases before the U.S. Supreme Court.